SUPERFOODS
GENETIC MODIFICATION OF FOODS
REVISED AND UPDATED

science at the edge

SALLY MORGAN

Heinemann Library
Chicago, Illinois

© 2009 Heinemann Library
an imprint of Capstone Global Library, LLC
Chicago, Illinois

Customer service 888-454-2279

Visit our website at www.heinemannraintree.com

Printed and bound in China by South China Printing Company Ltd.

13 12 11 10 09
10 9 8 7 6 5 4 3 2 1

New edition ISBN: 978 1 4329 2455 3 (hardcover)

The Library of Congress has cataloged the first edition as follows:
Morgan, Sally.
    Superfoods : genetic modification of foods / Sally Morgan.
        p.   cm.—(Science at the edge)
    Includes bibliographical references and index.
    ISBN 1-58810-702-7 (HC), 1-4034-4123-5 (Pbk.)
    ISBN 978-1-58810-702-2 (HC), 978-1-4034-4123-2 (Pbk.)
    I. Genetically modified foods—Juvenile literature. [I. Genetically modified foods. 2. Food--Biotechnology.] I. Title. II. Series.
    TP248.65.F66 .M67 2002
    363.19'29--dc21

Acknowledgments
The author and publishers are grateful to the following for permission to reproduce copyright material:
© Alamy p. **4** (Jenny Matthews); © Corbis pp. **39** (Jim Richardson), **42** (Pete Leonard/Zefa), **49**; © Ecoscene pp. **5**, **11**, **12**, **13**, **31**, **37** (David McHugh), **50** (Chinch Gryniewicz), **51**, **53**, **54**; © Getty Images p. **34**; © Popperfoto p. **29** (Reuters); © Science Photo Library pp. **20** (Alfred Pasieka), **21** (Rosenfeld Images Ltd), **25** (P. Dumas/Eurelios), **26** (Chris Knapton), **28** (CC Studio), **32** (PH. Plailly/Eurelios), **35** (Steve Woit/AGStockUSA), **40** (Sheila Terry), **44** (Adam Hart-Davis), **46** (Debra Ferguson/AGStockUSA), **48**; © Still Pictures p. **56** (Mark Edwards).

Cover photograph of scientist with plants reproduced with permission of © Getty Images/Zomi.

CONTENTS

Some words are printed in bold, **like this**. You can find out what they mean by looking in the glossary.

INTRODUCTION

Each year up to 500,000 children in the developing world go blind because they do not have enough Vitamin A in their diet. Eating a couple of carrots a day would solve the problem, but there are no carrots grown in these countries. By 2012 these children will be able to eat a special type of rice, called golden rice, that has been genetically modified to contain enough Vitamin A to stop them going blind.

Helping to Feed the World

Malnutrition is just one of the challenges in feeding the world's population. At the turn of the millennium, the human population stood at just more than 6 billion. By 2030 the world population is expected to be more than 8.2 billion people, a 36 percent increase in just 30 years. This massive increase means that governments will have to solve problems such as hunger and poverty, while also protecting the world's natural environment.

Meeting all of these challenges will require new scientific knowledge and the development of new technologies, such as genetic modification, also known as genetic engineering. This promising technology involves changing the genetic content of plants and animals in order to create foods with new characteristics.

In south Sudan malnutrition is common. Here a mother waits with her child for food during a famine. The hope is that genetic modification can help people like this.

New Crops

During the last 15 years, scientists have created a range of new genetically modified (GM) crops. Today, the four main GM crops are soybean, cotton, rapeseed, and corn, which are commonly grown in countries such as the United States, Canada, China, India, Brazil, and South Africa. These crops are beginning to change the face of agriculture. However, this change is not welcomed by everyone. In the late 1990s and early 2000s, protestors destroyed GM crop testing in parts of Europe, and there were protests outside supermarkets selling GM foods. Newspapers carried stories about "Frankenstein" foods and genetic "nightmares." This contributed to a widespread public rejection in Europe of genetic modifications and the developments linked to it.

In this book you can read about **DNA** and discover how scientists can alter DNA through genetic engineering. You can find out how people are improving crops and livestock through a process called artificial selection and how this process can be speeded up by using genetic engineering. Many types of genetically altered organisms and foods containing GM products are sold to the public. You can decide for yourself whether GM technology is a good or bad thing and if foods containing GM products are safe to eat.

Each year farmers in the United States plant GM crops, such as this field of corn.

"I have absolutely no anxiety. I am worried by a lot of things, but not about modified food."

Dr. James Watson, winner of the Nobel Prize for his work on DNA

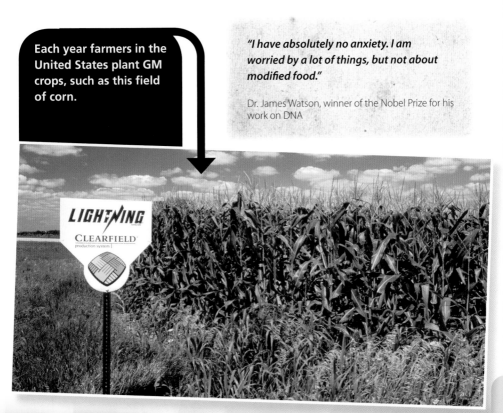

UNDERSTANDING GENES

Every organism carries within it a set of instructions that control all the processes in its cells. The instructions are in the form of codes, and they are stored in the **genes**. The genes themselves are made of DNA (deoxyribonucleic acid).

Genetic engineering is the deliberate alteration of an organism's genes in order to give it new abilities. For example, some bacteria have been given the gene to make the human **protein** insulin. Insulin is a substance that controls the level of glucose in the blood. The term genetically modified organism (GMO) is used to describe a plant, animal, or microorganism that has had its DNA altered in some way by genetic engineering.

Early Genetics

Our understanding of genetics dates back to the time of Gregor Mendel, a scientist who carried out experiments using peas during the 1860s. In one experiment he crossed tall peas with dwarf peas and found that all the offspring were tall. He concluded that the features of the two parents did not simply blend together to produce medium height peas. Instead the feature of one parent, in this case the tall parent, always appeared in the offspring, while the other feature did not appear—it was masked.

Mendel's work formed the basis of modern genetics. He discovered the laws of inheritance without having any knowledge of cell structure or biochemistry. It was only at the beginning of the 20th century, when more powerful microscopes were invented, that biologists were able to study the actual genetic material found in the **nucleus**—the **chromosomes**. It was not until the 1920s that the substance that makes up the chromosomes—DNA—was discovered.

DNA Structure

The key breakthrough in the understanding of genetics came in 1953, when scientists Francis Crick and James Watson, with help from Rosalind Franklin, determined the structure of the DNA **molecule**. Since then, our knowledge of DNA and the **genetic code** has improved dramatically. This knowledge has enabled scientists to alter DNA and transfer it between organisms.

DNA is a long molecule that consists of two strands twisted around each other to form a spiral called a helix. It can be likened to a twisted ladder: the sides of the ladder are made from alternating sugar and phosphate molecules, and the rungs are formed by molecules known as bases. There are four different bases in DNA: adenine (A), guanine (G), cytosine (C), and thymine (T). A and G are large molecules, while C and T molecules are smaller ones. Each rung consists of one large molecule joined to a small one, so that the width is always the same. A always pairs with T, and C always pairs with G. It is the order of bases along a strand of DNA that forms a genetic code.

FOCUS Discovering the Double Helix

Probably the most exciting and significant biological discovery of the 20th century was solving the structure of DNA. In 1953 Francis Crick and James Watson published the details of their proposed structure of DNA. It had been known for some time that DNA was made up of sugar, phosphate, and the four bases—adenine, guanine, cytosine, and thymine—but nobody knew how these components were joined together. One key part of the puzzle was provided by Edwin Chargaff. During the late 1940s, his research had found that the number of guanine bases equalled the number of cytosine bases and, similarly, the number of adenine bases equalled the number of thymine bases. After this, Maurice Wilkins and Rosalind Franklin took an X-ray of DNA, which showed that it formed a helix. Finally, Crick and Watson studied all the evidence and decided that DNA in fact formed a double helix.

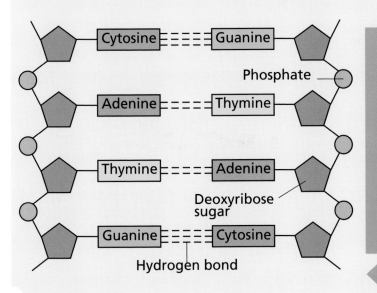

Cytosine ===== Guanine

Phosphate

Adenine ==== Thymine

Thymine ==== Adenine

Deoxyribose sugar

Guanine ==== Cytosine

Hydrogen bond

DNA is made up of sugar and phosphate molecules together with four different types of bases. The two strands of DNA are held together by weak bonds called hydrogen bonds.

7

Genes and Simple Genetics

Genes control the manufacture of proteins in a cell. There are thousands of different genes, each responsible for making a specific protein. In a human cell there are two copies of each gene, one inherited from the father and the other from the mother. Genes can exist in two forms, called alleles. One allele is described as being dominant and the other as being recessive. The dominant allele will usually mask the appearance of the recessive allele. A person can have two dominant alleles, one dominant and one recessive, or two recessive.

For example, humans can have brown eyes or blue eyes. The dominant allele codes for brown pigment in eyes, and the recessive allele codes for blue eyes. To have brown eyes, a person must inherit at least one allele for brown eyes. This means that both of the alleles could be brown or just one. The outward appearance is always the same—brown eyes. To have blue eyes a person must have two blue-eye alleles—in other words, they must inherit a blue-eye allele from each parent. This is a very simplified explanation of inheritance. In reality, most characteristics are controlled by several genes working together.

FOCUS Inheriting Genes

In this diagram, B represents the allele for brown eyes, and b represents the allele for blue eyes. (Remember, a person inherits one allele from each parent.) If a brown-eyed person (BB) with two brown-eye alleles reproduces with a person with blue eyes (bb), all their children will have brown eyes.

They will all have one brown-eye allele and one blue-eye allele (Bb). The blue-eye allele is masked by the brown-eye allele. If one of these children reproduces with a person with the same alleles, there are three possible outcomes: BB, Bb, and bb. Three out of four children will have brown eyes (BB and Bb), and one out of four will have blue eyes (bb).

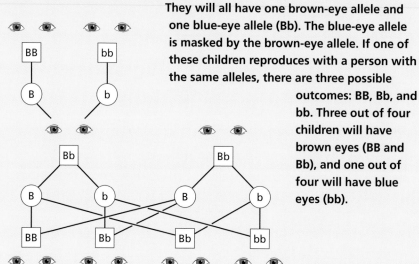

Recombinant DNA

In 1970 researchers discovered **enzymes** that could cut DNA at specific points. These enzymes were essential to the process of cutting out a length of DNA and pasting it into the DNA of another organism. Through this process, scientists created **recombinant DNA**, which is DNA made up of one or more lengths from different organisms. The first successful transfer of DNA took place in 1973. During the 1980s the first **transgenic** animals and plants appeared. These were organisms that contained genetic material that had been artificially inserted from another species.

During the 1990s a wide range of genetically modified animals and plants were produced, followed by the appearance of GM foods in supermarkets. It was at this stage that the first concerns about GM foods started to appear.

Key Players

GM plants and animals are created by a wide range of international **biotechnology** companies and research institutes. Before a GMO may be used commercially, it has to be approved by government food agencies, such as the Food and Drug Administration (FDA). In addition, international organizations, such as the Food and Agriculture Organization (FAO), provide advice and guidance to governments and help to determine international standards for GM foods.

 FOCUS ## The Food and Agriculture Organization (FAO)

The FAO was established in 1945 as an independent organization of the **United Nations**. Its role is to promote agricultural development and to improve the nutritional standards of rural populations. It aims to provide all people with access to the food they require for an active and healthy life. The FAO offers direct development assistance; collects, analyzes, and distributes information; provides policy and planning advice to governments; and acts as an international forum for debate on food and agricultural issues. In 1963 the FAO and the World Health Organization formed the **Codex Alimentarius Commission**, which is responsible for the international food code that covers food production and food safety. During the past 10 years, the commission has been evaluating GM foods and the risk they pose to human health. The standards published by the commission do not have to be adopted by national governments, but the World Trade Organization refers to these standards when there are trade disputes between nations.

IMPROVING PLANTS AND ANIMALS

The breeding of plants and animals has produced higher-yielding crops, plants with better insect and disease **resistance**, larger animals for meat, and dairy cows that produce significantly more milk each year than their predecessors.

First Farmers

People who lived 20,000 years ago or more were hunter-gatherers. They moved from place to place, hunting animals and collecting fruits and nuts from the wild. Eventually, people started to grow their own crops. They sowed seeds collected from wild grasses, and at the end of the growing season they harvested crops and new seeds. They soon learned to save the seeds from the plants that gave the best yields because this would produce a better crop next time. As a result of this selection process, the yields increased greatly.

Natural Selection v. Artificial Selection

Natural selection is one of the processes through which evolution occurs. In any group of individuals of the same species, there will be a few that are better adapted to an environment than others. The best adapted individuals survive and breed, passing on their genes to offspring. This is often called "survival of the fittest."

FOCUS **Evolution of Wheat**

Wheat can be traced back to wild grasses that were growing thousands of years ago. These grasses had cells that contained 14 chromosomes. The different types of wild grasses were grown together and, by chance, a hybrid plant was produced. This grass had 28 chromosomes, double the original number. It was a far more vigorous plant and had larger seeds. Thousands of years later, another lucky crossing produced the modern wheat plant, which has 42 chromosomes. Recently, a new cereal called triticale has been produced by crossbreeding durum wheat (*Triticum*) with rye (*Secale*). Triticale is a versatile cereal with a high yield and hardiness, so it can grow in harsh climates.

Imagine several plants from the same species that have prickly leaves. The individual plants that have more prickly leaves are less likely to be eaten by grazing animals than those that have just a few prickles. The more prickly plants survive and produce seeds that grow into plants that also have more prickles. Over time, the less prickly plants disappear, and the more prickly ones increase.

Farmers have replaced this kind of natural selection with artificial selection, or selection based on a human decision. If this species of plant was good to eat, it is easy to imagine that a farmer would have chosen to grow the less-prickly plants. The farmer would have kept grazing animals separate from the plants, so it would not matter that the plants were more vulnerable to animals. Gradually, the plants would become less prickly. In this case the farmer has "selected" certain genes.

A similar process has occurred with animals. The first animals to be domesticated were herd animals, which could be rounded up and kept in corrals (fenced-off areas). Early farmers bred from the smaller animals, which were easier to handle and did not eat as much as the larger ones. Today, farmers breed domesticated animals for size, muscle, and milk production.

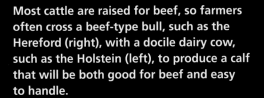
Most cattle are raised for beef, so farmers often cross a beef-type bull, such as the Hereford (right), with a docile dairy cow, such as the Holstein (left), to produce a calf that will be both good for beef and easy to handle.

Characteristics of Artificial Selection

The process of artificial selection is slow, especially with animals. Some animals take several years to mature and only produce one offspring at a time. The process can also be hit-and-miss. Farmers try to choose parents with care, bringing together animals with desirable features, for example a ewe and a ram that both have good-quality wool. But there is no guarantee that two sheep with quality wool will produce offspring with equally good or better wool. Sometimes the combination of features in an offspring can actually make a certain characteristic worse, rather than better.

Results from artificial selection can be seen more quickly in plants. First, the parent plants with the desirable characteristics are identified. Pollen is removed from the flowers of one plant and used to **pollinate** the flowers of another. Since plants generally produce many seeds, all the seeds are **germinated** and the new plants are examined to see if there has been any improvement.

MUTATIONS

Sometimes a completely new variation appears in the genetic material of an offspring. These sudden changes are called mutations. Many mutations are harmful to an organism and it does not survive, but occasionally they are useful and the animal or plant passes on the mutation to their offspring. Some mutations have greatly improved a crop or animal.

A high yielding variety of wheat has a short stalk that is less susceptible to lodging (bending over after wind and rain). It also produces an "ear" or seed head with many seeds that swell in size and ripen ready for harvest at the same time.

For example, the seed stalk in wild grasses shatters easily in order to disperse its seeds. Early in the history of wheat, a **mutant** appeared that had a strong seed stalk. This was a real bonus to farmers, as the seeds stayed attached to the plant and could be collected. This mutation would have been disastrous in a wild grass because the plant would have been unable to spread its seeds, but it worked well for farmers.

SMART BREEDING

Traditional selective breeding techniques have been updated, and a natural form of plant breeding called SMART breeding (Selection with Markers and Advanced Reproductive Technologies) is emerging. This technique is possible becauase of improved knowledge of plant genes and where they occur on the chromosome, but it does not actually involve genetic engineering. SMART breeding was established by an Israeli scientist named Nachum Kedar, who crossed varieties of tomato to produce a high-yielding tomato plant with tomatoes that would ripen on the vine and have a longer shelf life. Now scientists are applying this technique to other crops, such as wheat and rice.

> *"We're finding things like genes in low-yielding wild ancestors, which if you move them into cultivated varieties can increase the yields of the best cultivar. We also have ways to make larger seeds, which can yield bigger fruit."*
>
> Susan McCouch, Cornell University, who is crossbreeding modern varieties of rice with wild ancestors to produce high-yielding new varieties

Scientist have produced a map of the genes in rice. This information can be used by research institutes, such as this one at Hyderabad in India where researchers are studying the resistance of different rice varieties to the white-backed plant hopper, a major insect pest.

GENETIC CHANGES

Traditional **selective breeding** methods are based on the transfer of genetic material between individuals of the same species. Some genetic engineering is not that different from selective breeding, but it is a far more rapid and precise process. However, genetic engineering also makes it possible to move genes between species that would not normally interbreed, which is something that cannot usually be achieved through selective breeding.

Transgenic Organisms

Plants and animals that contain foreign DNA are called transgenics. For example, sheep that have been given an extra gene to make a substance that is normally made by humans are transgenic because they contain human DNA. The change in the sheep's DNA means that it is different from other animals of the same type—it is a new strain.

Organisms that receive a new gene have new abilities. For example, they may be able to make a new protein or enzyme, or produce a substance, such as an **antibiotic**. It is this feature that makes the technique of genetic engineering revolutionary, because it has great potential benefits.

The following are some of the advantages that genetic engineering has over selective breeding:

- The desired change can be achieved in very few generations.
- It is faster and lower in cost.
- It allows greater precision in selecting certain characteristics.
- It allows a much wider selection of traits for improvement. In plants, for example, it can introduce pest, disease, drought, and herbicide resistance in addition to improved nutritional content.

Making Proteins

Proteins are essential building blocks and have many functions in the body. Hemoglobin, for example, is an oxygen-carrying protein in the blood. Keratin, in the skin, nails, and hair, is a structural protein.

Each gene is responsible for the manufacture of a specific protein. For example, one gene carries the instructions for a specific type of blood protein, while another is responsible for making the brown pigment found in skin, hair, and eyes. All proteins are made from **amino acids**.

There are 20 different amino acids, and it is the composition of these and the order in which they occur that determines the type of protein they form.

If a gene mutates in some way, its genetic code may be changed. This means that cells may not be able to make a particular protein, and the body suffers from a malfunction. A single faulty gene causes the disease cystic fibrosis, which affects the lungs and digestive system.

FOCUS Protein Synthesis

The process of making a protein begins when part of a DNA molecule in the nucleus unwinds to expose the bases. The genetic code is formed from groups of three bases. Each group of three bases identifies a specific amino acid. There are 64 possible combinations of the four bases: A, T, G, and C. Because there are only 20 amino acids, some amino acids have more than one code, while others are used to indicate the start and finish of the message.

A messenger molecule (**RNA**) is used to carry the information from the DNA in the nucleus to the **cytoplasm**. Here, the RNA attaches to a tiny structure called a ribosome and the code is read, one group of three bases at a time. The corresponding amino acids are picked up from the cytoplasm and joined together in the correct order. This forms a strand of amino acids that makes up new protein.

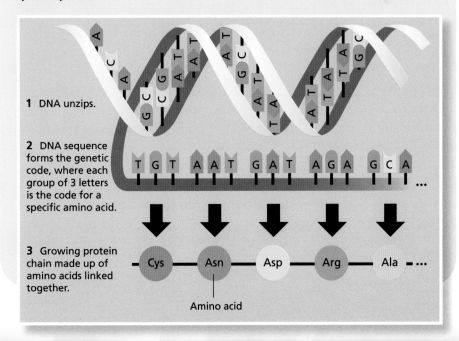

1 DNA unzips.

2 DNA sequence forms the genetic code, where each group of 3 letters is the code for a specific amino acid.

T G T   A A T   G A T   A G A   G C A ...

3 Growing protein chain made up of amino acids linked together.

Cys — Asn — Asp — Arg — Ala ...

Amino acid

The Process of Genetic Engineering

The first stage in genetic engineering is to identify the desired gene on the DNA of the donor organism. Once located, the gene has to be "cut out" and then "pasted" into another piece of DNA, which will be inserted into the recipient organism. DNA that contains foreign DNA is known as recombinant DNA.

MOLECULAR SCISSORS

Scientists use special enzymes to cut DNA into many small pieces. These enzymes act like molecular scissors. There are thousands of different special enzymes, each of which cuts at a specific point on the DNA. These enzymes make it easier to find and remove individual genes. Now it is possible to remove a specific length of DNA from one organism and insert it into the DNA of another.

Before the selected length of DNA can be pasted into the new DNA, it has to be copied billions of times to produce enough material. This takes place in a solution containing a specific mix of chemicals.

INSERTING THE DNA

Once a length of DNA has been copied it has to be inserted into the host cell. Some animal cells take up new DNA by simply injecting it into their nucleus. First, the new DNA is attached to a length of DNA that has been taken from the animal cell, so the cell will recognize it. Then the new DNA and the DNA to which it is attached get stitched into the host cell's own DNA.

In bacteria, a circular piece of DNA, called a plasmid, found in the cytoplasm, is used to get the DNA into the host bacterium. The desired gene is first stitched into the plasmid, and then the plasmid is inserted into the bacterium.

The cells of plants, however, are surrounded by a thick cell wall. In order to introduce the new DNA, some plants are genetically modified using natural plant parasites. One type of soil bacterium, for example, has a natural ability to transfer its own genes into a plant, and could be called nature's own genetic engineer. This bacterium is used by geneticists (scientists who study genetics) to insert other genes of interest.

Cereals are genetically modified using a gene gun. The gun fires tungsten (a type of metal) particles coated in DNA at the plant. The particles penetrate the plant cell wall and some enter the nucleus, where the foreign DNA becomes incorporated into the cell's own DNA.

FOCUS Genetically Engineered Chymosin

Cheese is traditionally made using rennet. Rennet is essential to cheese production because it curdles the milk, separating it into solid curds and liquid whey. The curds are pressed to make cheese. Natural rennet is obtained from the stomachs of young calves—the rennet contains an enzyme that enables the animal to digest milk. However, because rennet is taken from animals, many people, including vegetarians, do not eat traditionally manufactured cheese. Now an artificial rennet containing chymosin can be manufactured using genetically modified yeast.

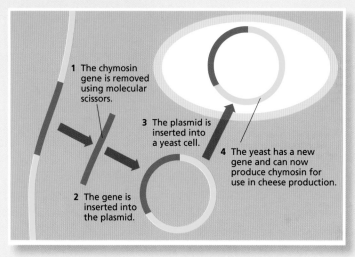

1 The chymosin gene is removed using molecular scissors.

2 The gene is inserted into the plasmid.

3 The plasmid is inserted into a yeast cell.

4 The yeast has a new gene and can now produce chymosin for use in cheese production.

The scientists who developed artificial rennet located the gene for chymosin on cow's DNA and removed it using specific molecular scissors. The DNA was cut in such a way that one strand of DNA was left longer than the other, creating what is called a "sticky end." A plasmid was cut open and the new DNA was added to one end. The ends were rejoined using another enzyme. This technique is called gene-splicing. The engineered plasmid was then inserted into a yeast cell, giving the yeast the ability to make chymosin. The plasmid remains within the yeast, and each time the yeast reproduces, the chymosin gene is passed on to a new generation of yeast.

Despite the fact that chymosin is a product of GM yeast, many vegetarian societies consider it a preferable source of rennet. Today chymosin makes up more than half of the world's supply of rennet. However, adverse publicity concerning GM foods during the late 1990s led to cheese manufacturers seeking an alternative. A yeast has now been discovered that produces a chymosin-like substance naturally.

EXPRESSING ITSELF

Once inside a cell, the next problem is to get the gene to work, or to express itself. For example, if a geneticist has inserted a gene for producing a particular protein in seeds, they do not want the plant to instead produce the protein in its leaves. Chromosomes have control regions that switch certain genes on or off. So as well as being able to successfully insert a new gene, a geneticist has to be able to alter the control region so that the new gene is switched on in the places where it is required.

GENETIC MARKERS

Once DNA has been inserted into the DNA of another organism, the researchers need to prove that the process has been successful. This is achieved using marker genes that are attached to the target gene. One of the most common markers is a gene that makes the organism resistant to a specific antibiotic. To check that bacteria, for example, have been successfully modified, they are spread onto a plate of agar jelly, which contains the antibiotic ampicillin. The ampicillin will normally kill all the bacteria. Only those bacteria that contain the genetic marker gene will be able to grow and reproduce. These cells can be isolated and cultured to produce more bacteria. The bacteria are then modified again to remove the marker gene. Some of the early GM corn plants contained a marker gene that gave resistance to ampicillin. If the plant showed resistance to ampicillin, it also contained the gene for resistance to an insect called the corn borer.

There are other types of genetic marker. A type of jellyfish exists that glows green in the dark. The gene that causes this has been identified and removed. It can be attached to other genes and inserted into a different organism. In this case scientists can tell the modification has been successful when the organism glows green!

> "Understanding cereal genetic structure and associated proteins will enable plant breeders to produce crops that are more nutritious, more productive, and easier to process. We will also research new ways to protect crops from diseases or pests and discover new uses for crop plants. This offers exciting new opportunities to improve agricultural yields and quality."
>
> Dr. David Evans, former head of research and technology at Syngenta, now a member of the SCI BioResources Group

The Rice Genome

In January 2001 the biotechnology company Syngenta announced that it had completed the rice **genome** map. The company's researchers had determined the complete DNA sequence—the exact order of the bases (cytosine, guanine, thymine, and adenine)—along a DNA strand in rice, as well as identifying some of the sequences that control gene activity and the location of most of the genes. A more detailed analysis of gene activity and function and the resulting proteins is in progress. Rice has 12 chromosomes and 50,000 genes. This adds up to 430 million base pairs on the DNA. Rice is similar to other cereals, so the information gained from rice will contribute to the study of cereals such as wheat, corn, and barley and lead to their future improvement. Rice is a vital crop in the developing world, and Syngenta promises that it will work with local research institutes to explore how this information can best be used to find crop improvements to benefit **subsistence farmers**.

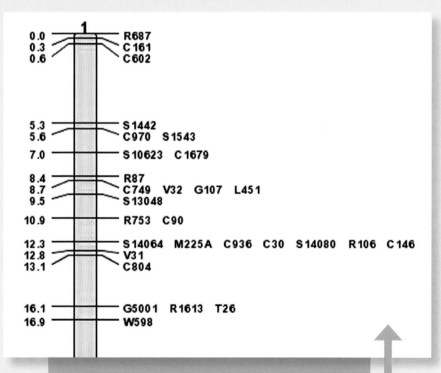

Position	Genes
0.0	R687
0.3	C161
0.6	C602
5.3	S1442
5.6	C970 S1543
7.0	S10623 C1679
8.4	R87
8.7	C749 V32 G107 L451
9.5	S13048
10.9	R753 C90
12.3	S14064 M225A C936 C30 S14080 R106 C146
12.8	V31
13.1	C804
16.1	G5001 R1613 T26
16.9	W598

This is a genetic map of part of chromosome 1 of the rice plant. The lines show the position and name of the genes as they occur along the DNA. Chromosome 1 is the largest of the 12 chromosomes in rice and is expected to have about 7,000 genes.

Cloning

Successfully modifying the DNA of an organism takes time and luck. Once achieved, scientists have to find ways to produce more of the organism without altering the DNA again. They need **clones**. Bacteria and yeast increase in number by simply dividing in two. A new cell is an exact copy of the parent cell. Therefore, genetically modified bacteria and yeast are easy to reproduce because the DNA remains the same.

Genetically modified plants have to be **propagated** asexually using cuttings or tissue culture. For example, a length of shoot can be taken from a GM plant and treated in such a way that it grows roots. The new plant is identical to the parent. Or plants can be reproduced from tiny samples of tissue. The sample is placed in a **growth medium**, which causes the cells to grow shoots and roots. Seeds cannot be used because they are produced through sexual reproduction. Pollen from one plant pollinates a flower on another plant, which then develops seeds. The seeds contain genes from both parents, which means that the resulting plants will be different from both parents.

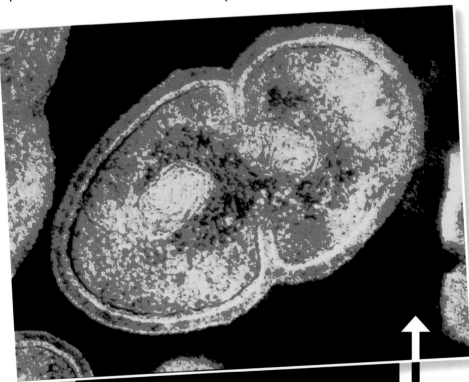

Organisms such as bacteria and yeast reproduce by simply dividing in two. This is called binary fission. The two new cells are identical to each other.

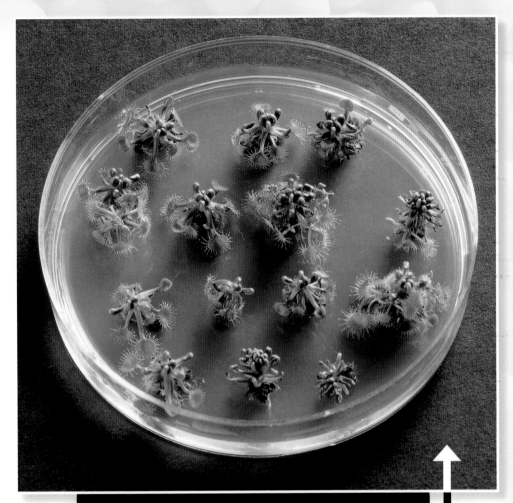

These tiny sundew plants are identical copies of the parent plant. Several samples of cells were taken from the parent and placed on a growth medium. The growth medium contains carefully controlled quantities of plant growth substances, which cause new shoots and roots to form.

Mammals are far more complex and difficult to clone, but the cloning of animals does occur naturally—for example, identical twins are clones of each other. A **fertilized** egg can split in two, and two **embryos** develop instead of one. Each embryo has the same genetic composition. Currently, the most common way to clone a mammal artificially is to take an egg cell, remove its nucleus, and replace it with a nucleus taken from a genetically modified mammal. The egg is stimulated so that it divides and develops into a new individual (see page 28).

NEW CROPS

A range of GM crops has been developed over the past 15 years. Today, 114 million hectares (282 million acres) of farmland is used to grow them worldwide, up from 40 million hectares (100 million acres) in 2000. GM crops are grown commercially in 23 countries, including the United States, Argentina, Brazil, and Canada. The main crops are soybeans, corn, cotton, and rapeseed.

As described in the previous chapter, genetic engineering offers a number of advantages over traditional **selective breeding**. These advantages could lead to a number of benefits:

- better yields while using fewer pesticides

- an ability to grow crops in previously inhospitable environments, because of the increased ability of plants to grow in conditions of drought, salinity (saltiness), and extremes of temperature

- improved sensory attributes of food, for example, flavor and texture

- better nutritional content, for example, increased Vitamin A content in rice, or removal of the factors that cause allergies to certain foods, such as nuts

- easier processing that leads to reduced waste and lower food costs for the consumer.

Pesticides

Pests can devastate crops. They eat plant leaves, reducing crop yield and quality. In all parts of the world, pests can be highly damaging. Locusts, for example, can consume an entire crop in just a few hours. As a result, farmers have to protect their crops by using pesticides. Most pesticides are chemicals that kill either a specific pest or a range of pests. Insecticides are used to kill insect pests, while fungicides are used on fungal pests. Herbicides kill unwanted plants or weeds. Some herbicides, such as glyphosate and paraquat, kill all plants with which they come into contact. Others just kill only plants with narrow leaves such as grasses, or plants with broad leaves such as dock and thistles.

Pesticides have some advantages. They are fast acting, generally reliable, and can be applied with ease. But there are disadvantages, too. Pesticides are expensive to buy and require the use of specialized equipment. Many pesticides kill insects indiscriminately, destroying useful as well as harmful insects. For example, some pesticides kill both the greenfly and its natural predator, the ladybug. Most modern pesticides are designed to break down once they have been in the soil for a few weeks, so that they do not remain in the environment. However, heavy a rainfall shortly after spraying can wash off the pesticide, forcing a farmer to respray. The runoff can drain into streams, rivers, and lakes, where the pesticides harm aquatic life. Pesticides do not kill all pests they target, so they usually have to be reapplied. For example, in the southern United States, cotton may be sprayed up to eight times a year, but up to 15 percent of the crop may still be lost to pests. Finally, there are fears that residue from pesticides that remains on food crops may harm the health of consumers.

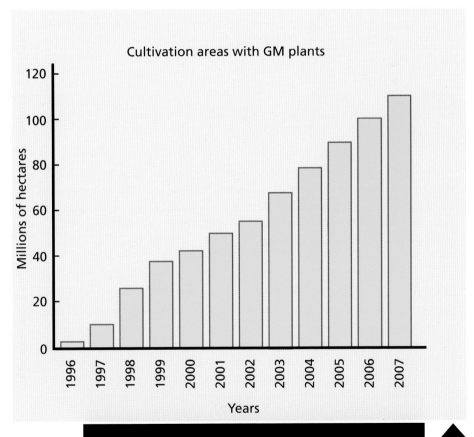

This graph shows how the cultivation of genetically modified crops has grown worldwide since 1996, when only a relatively small amount of land was used for GM crops.

Pesticide Resistance

Among the first genetically engineered plants were those that had been given built-in resistance to pests. One gene of particular interest is found in the soil bacterium *Bacillus thuringiensis,* known as Bt. This bacterium produces a selective **toxin** that is poisonous to most insects, especially caterpillars, but harmless to most other organisms. An organic insecticide can be made by growing Bt bacteria and then drying them to form a powder that contains the poison, but the powder is difficult to use and is not always effective. The gene that makes the toxin has been identified, removed, and inserted into crop plants such as corn, cabbage, and cotton. Cotton plants have been given this gene so that they can produce the toxin to kill the cotton bollworm. These cotton varieties are grown in eight countries, where they make up more than 40 percent of the total cotton crop. However, there is still much debate as to whether the crops are higher yielding and require less spraying.

FOCUS Wildlife Concerns

Many conservationists are concerned that the use of herbicide-resistant crops could lead to farmers using more herbicides, which could wipe out plants that are beneficial to wildlife. In 1999 the United Kingdom asked an independent team of researchers to carry out extensive field testing on three GM crops resistant to herbicides, GM corn, rapeseed, and sugar beet, to discover how the GM crops affected the diversity and abundance of wildlife on farms compared to conventional crops. The researchers looked at the way weeds grew around crops and studied the animals that fed on the weeds. They discovered that conventional sugar beets and spring-sown rapeseed supported more wildlife, especially bees and butterflies, than the GM equivalent did. There were more weed seeds, a valuable food source for birds, on the conventional crops, too. GM corn supported more weeds, and there was no difference between GM winter rapeseed and the conventional one. The results of these tests, together with public resistance to the use of GM crops, has meant that no GM crops have been approved for commercial use in the United Kingdom, and only one crop test, for GM potatoes, is under way. In France a ban on GM crops was put in place starting in December 2007.

Stay-Fresh Vegetables

As well as giving crops resistance to disease and pests, some crop modifications are aimed at improving the shelf life of vegetables, especially salad ingredients, which spoil quickly on supermarket shelves and create a lot of waste. One way to increase the shelf life is to slow down the ripening process, so producers have more time to get their vegetables into supermarkets. The ripening process involves an enzyme called pectinase. This enzyme breaks down the pectin that holds plant cells together. When this happens, the fruit or vegetable softens. Researchers have targeted this enzyme in the tomato. They removed the gene and replaced it in the opposite direction. This simple procedure switched off the gene and prevented the enzyme from being made. The altered tomatoes ripened more slowly. They remained firm for much longer, were easier to handle, and there was much less waste.

A scientist monitors the uptake of oxygen by a melon plant. The melons have been modified so that they ripen more slowly, giving them a longer shelf life.

Herbicide Resistance

Glyphosate is a widely used and relatively cheap, nonselective herbicide. It kills most of the plants with which it comes into contact, but it does not stay in the soil. It works well as a garden weed killer used by targeting specific plants, but it cannot be used on crops because it would kill them. Now there are GM crops, including soybeans, that have a gene from a bacterium that gives them resistance to glyphosate. Soybeans are grown widely in the United States and Brazil. They are an important source of protein and are used in processed foods and animal feeds. Before the arrival of the GM soybean, farmers who grew soybeans could only use selective herbicides, which were expensive and often stayed in the ground for many months. Now they can use the cheaper and more environmentally-friendly glyphosate-resistant soybean. The GM soybean is just one of several herbicide-resistant crop plants. Varieties of corn, sugar beet, and rapeseed have all been modified to give them resistance to certain types of herbicide.

Weeds growing among crop plants compete with them for water, nutrients, and space. If weeds are not removed, the crop yield will be reduced. Now it is possible to spray GM corn plants with the weed killer glyphosate to kill all the weeds without harming the crop. The dead weeds form a layer over the soil that traps moisture, which also helps the crop.

Problems with Approval

A number of new GM crops and other plants have been developed, but before they can be approved for use commercially, they need to undergo field testing and environmental reviews. The approval of new crops has been halted in the United States because a judge has ruled that the Department of Agriculture must conduct more stringent environmental reviews—and that some of the approvals in recent years were illegal.

FOCUS The Case of GM Creeping Bentgrass

GM varieties of creeping bentgrass and Kentucky bluegrass have been developed in the United States. These grasses are used in lawns and are resistant to herbicides. This allows people to spray herbicide on GM lawns to kill the weeds but not the grass. People fear that the widescale planting of these grasses will lead to much greater use of herbicides. There are also fears that the pollen from the grass could lead to the resistance being passed to other species of grasses. A court decision in the United States overturned the approval of the GM grasses until more rigorous field testing has been conducted.

The following table shows some of the crops with modified features that are currently undergoing field tests around the world.

CROP	MODIFIED FEATURE
Apple	Insect resistance
Banana	Plants that are free from viruses and worm parasites
Broccoli	Slow ripening, so flower head stays green longer and does not turn yellow
Cabbage	Resistance to attack by caterpillars
Celery	Retention of crispness
Coffee	Better flavor, yields, and pest resistance; lower caffeine content
Cucumber	Resistance to viruses, fungi, and bacteria
Melon	Extended shelf life
Potato	Resistance to caterpillars and beetles; lower fertilizer requirement; lower water content so less fat is absorbed in cooking process (low-fat French fries)
Raspberry	Increased sugar content; extended shelf life
Strawberry	Resistance to frost
Sunflower	More nutritious oils with lower saturated-fat content
Tomato	Resistance to viral diseases; increased yield; slow ripening; resistance to rotting after harvest; lower water content; frost resistance; increased sugar content
Wheat	Flour more suitable for bread-making; resistance to herbicide

GENETICALLY MODIFIED ANIMALS

Genetically modifying an animal, such as a fish, bird, or mammal, is far more complex than modifying bacteria or plants. A GM animal has to be altered while it is at the embryo stage. After fertilization, a cell starts to divide, and within a few days, it is a ball of cells. To ensure that all the cells contain the new DNA, a fertilized egg has to be altered before it divides. A length of DNA is removed from a donor organism and injected into the nucleus of the egg. It might become incorporated into the DNA, or it might not. The procedure is hit-and-miss—often it has to be carried out on hundreds of fertilized egg cells just to be successful with one or two.

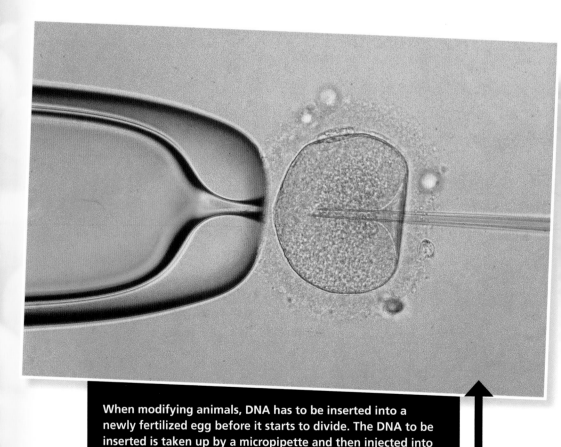

When modifying animals, DNA has to be inserted into a newly fertilized egg before it starts to divide. The DNA to be inserted is taken up by a micropipette and then injected into the nucleus of the egg.

Should Animals Be Genetically Modified?

Research is under way to genetically alter pigs, cattle, chickens, sheep, and fish. There are many potential benefits in GM animals. These include better growth rates, leaner meat, and disease resistance. There are now GM pigs that produce meat with high levels of omega-3 fatty acids and dairy cows that produce high-protein milk. In the future, it could be possible to produce animals that are resistant to diseases, too. However, there have been some unpleasant results. A pig that had been modified with a human growth hormone grew bigger and more quickly than usual, but it suffered from arthritis (swollen joints), developed ulcers, and was sterile. There is a still a lot of negative media coverage about GM animals, and governments have been reluctant to approve them for commercial use because the risks are still not understood. If transgenic animals are approved for commercial use, would you be happy to eat meat from an animal that had been genetically modified?

The first experiments aimed at producing genetically engineered animals were carried out on mice. Scientists injected DNA into the nucleus of a fertilized egg, and this DNA joined to one of the chromosomes to become a permanent part of the mouse's genetic makeup. The DNA contained a gene that enabled the mouse to grow much larger than normal. The altered egg was placed back inside the uterus of a female mouse and allowed to develop naturally. The mouse gave birth to a baby mouse that contained the new gene, and it grew to be much larger than normal.

The mouse on the right has been genetically altered so that it does not suffer from the weakening of muscles that usually occurs in old age. Information gained from experiments such as this help research into the disease muscular dystrophy.

Super Salmon

A genetically modified salmon developed in North America was one of the first GM animals ready to be released commercially. However, the commercial farming of this salmon is yet to be approved. These salmon have had genes from a flounder (a type of flat fish) inserted into their DNA. The new genes increase the salmon's growth rate by between 400 and 600 percent. Also, the fish have a slightly lower fat content than unmodified salmon, which would benefit the health of consumers.

The altered salmon do not grow any larger than normal, but reach full size much quicker and require less food to do so. For example, at 18 months the salmon are five times the size of an unmodified salmon of the same age, but have consumed up to 20 percent less food. This means the GM salmon is ready for harvest in less than a year rather than the normal three years. This development could cut the cost of rearing salmon by half and allow a more rapid production cycle.

Although salmon is the first animal to be altered on this level, many other types of commercial fish could be modified in the future, including trout, tilapia, and arctic char. Tilapia is an important source of protein in many parts of the world. The ability to produce more fish in less time could help to alleviate food shortages in some of the poorest countries of the world.

The Canadian company that has produced the salmon claims that all the salmon are infertile. However, organizations that are campaigning against the release of the salmon say that it is impossible to guarantee sterility. They are concerned that the modified salmon will escape from fish farms and interbreed with wild salmon, allowing the gene for faster growth to spread through the wild salmon population. One possibility is to make it compulsory to keep the fish in landlocked pens to keep salmon from escaping.

Another problem that has emerged is the fact that some of the salmon are deformed. This is probably a result of the fish growing so quickly. The states of Oregon and Washington are so concerned that they have banned any genetically modified fish.

> "We cannot seem to contain genetically modified corn or wheat. So what happens when these fish get out in the wild?"
>
> Zeke Grader of the Pacific Coast Federation of Fisherman's Associations

BST and More Milk

The hormone that affects growth rate and muscle production in cattle is called bovine somatotrophin (BST). Farmers found that when they injected dairy cows with extra BST, the cows produced more milk and muscle. Originally the BST was taken from dead cows, but it can now be produced from genetically modified bacteria. It is called rBST (recombinant bovine somatotrophin), to distinguish it from the naturally produced hormone. A single dose of BST every two weeks can boost the milk yield of a cow by as much as 25 percent. However, there is a downside. So much energy is directed into producing milk that the animal is more likely to become ill. Cows receiving the treatment are more susceptible to udder infections and gut problems, and they often become lame. This means that the cow has to be given antibiotics and other medicines. It may even shorten her productive life. In 2008 as many as 30 percent of the dairy cows in the United States were injected with rBST. However, there is a growing consumer backlash against the use of the hormone. Some supermarkets have banned milk with the hormone and some milk cartons have "free from artificial growth hormones" written on them. Although the hormone continues to be used in the United States, it is banned in Europe, Japan, Australia, and most other developed countries.

The milk yield of every cow in a dairy is monitored and her diet is altered accordingly. This way, the diet can be optimized for maximum milk production. Injections of rBST increase milk yields even more.

Cloning Animals

At the moment, the only way to produce new transgenic animals is to alter the DNA in a normal embryo. This is an expensive procedure, so transgenic animals are very valuable. The next stage is to develop the procedure to clone these valuable animals. Clones are exact genetic copies of the original individual. Identical twins are clones. Identical twins result when a fertilized egg splits in two, and each of the cells grows into a new individual. The genetic material in each of the individuals is the same.

FOCUS   Dolly, the First Manufactured Clone

In 1996 Dolly the sheep was born. Her birth represented an important milestone in the field of genetics, because she was the first clone of an adult mammalian cell. The procedure involved taking an udder cell from an adult ewe. The nucleus was removed from the udder cell and placed inside an empty egg cell that had been taken from another ewe. The egg cell was stimulated so that it started to divide to produce an embryo. This embryo was placed inside the uterus of another sheep who actually gave birth to Dolly. Dolly was a clone of the ewe that had donated the udder cell.

This procedure proved that it was possible to clone mammals such as sheep, although hundreds of unsuccessful attempts were made before Dolly was produced. Since then clones of other mammals have been created, too, for example, goats, cows, pigs, horses, and dogs.

Dolly died from lung disease when she was just six years old, which is young for a sheep. The disease is more common in older sheep, so it is possible that she suffered from premature aging.

Cloned Dairy Cows

In 2001 a biotechnology company produced healthy clones of a dairy cow. Zita was a top-ranking Holstein dairy cow in the United States. Her daughters were also top-ranking cows, producing much more milk than other Holsteins. However, every time one of these top cows was mated with a bull, there was a chance that the offspring would not be productive like their mother. The only way to ensure that all future generations would be equally productive was to clone Zita. Cells were taken from Zita before she died and used to produce clones. Although these clones were identical to Zita, they were not recordbreaking milk producers.

At present, the success rate is low, and many clones are born with abnormalities or they die shortly after birth. In time the technique may improve, and it may become a relatively easy process to produce clones of cows, bulls, and genetically modified animals.

DISCUSS Are We Playing God?

Do you think that scientists are "playing God" when they alter animals? Is genetically modifying animals so that they can make drugs or produce more food turning them into instruments or "living drug factories"? Some people think this is ethically unacceptable.

However, it is important to remember that people have been changing animals through selective breeding ever since they were first domesticated. Modern breeds of livestock and pets are very different from the original wild species. They are kept in conditions different from those experienced in the wild. If released, they would probably not survive, because they have become so dependent on people for food. Genetic engineering is similar to selective breeding, except that it can be achieved more quickly.

There is also concern about the welfare of transgenic animals. However, the fact that an animal is transgenic does not itself create problems. Instead, it is the effect that a new gene may or may not have on the physical or psychological state of the animal that is important. It is this aspect that some animal welfare groups are exploring.

CHANGES TO OUR FOOD

Although there is some public discussion about the genetic modification of animals, it is the use of GM products in our food that has probably raised the greatest concerns among the public. More than 40 different GM crops have been approved for use in food in the United States. In the European Union, only three products—GM soybean, corn, and tomato paste—have been approved for sale, and no new GM crops have been approved by the European Union since April 1998. So how are these products used, and what are the concerns?

Processed Foods

Most processed foods contain ingredients derived from plants such as soybean, corn, rapeseed, and sugar beet. GM varieties exist of all of these plants. Soybeans are high in **protein**, so they are used in high-protein animal feed and in food for humans. Soybeans are added to food as a binding agent, stabilizer, and emulsifier. Binding agents make different ingredients stick together, and emulsifiers prevent the separation of oils and water in foods such as sauces and margarine.

In fact, soybean-based ingredients are found in more than 60 percent of processed foods, including bread, infant formula, cereals, soups, pasta, pizza, frozen meals, meat products, flour, ice cream, potato chips, chocolate, soy sauce, tofu, soy milk, and pet foods. Soybean oil and rapeseed oil are also used in foods that include vegetable fats

Soybeans are in high demand. Here, a factory worker empties boiled soybeans on a production line in Japan, where fermented soybeans are especially popular.

The pink color of this corn seed shows that is has been sprayed with fungicide and is ready for planting.

or hydrogenated fats. Soybean oil can be processed to make lecithin. Lecithin binds water and fats together and is used as a thickening agent in milkshakes, cookies, and chocolate bars. The first commercial harvest of GM soybeans in the United States occurred in 1996, and it quickly appeared in foods. Now GM varieties make up just over 90 percent of the soybean harvest in the United States.

Corn is also used in many processed foods, breads, and cereals. Corn-based ingredients that may appear on food labels include modified starch, cornflour, cornstarch, corn oil, corn syrup, dextrose, glucose, and polenta. Corn is used in animal feed, too. GM corn is grown commercially in the United States, where it currently makes up 73 percent of the total harvest. Corn is the only GM crop grown in parts of Europe, particularly in Spain, with smaller amounts in Germany, Portugal, and the Czech Republic. GM corn, however, represents less than two percent of the corn grown in Europe.

Rapeseed is widely used in vegetable (canola) oil, margarine, French fries, canned foods, processed foods, and snack foods. Although GM rapeseed is found in food in North America, it has not been approved for sale in the European Union. It is possible that foods imported from North America contain GM rapeseed.

Sugar comes from sugar beets and sugar cane, both of which have GM varieties. GM sugar beets are grown in China and South Africa. GM sugar could be used in processed foods.

The Approval Process

When introducing any new technology, including gene technology, into the food chain, it is essential to put in place appropriate safeguards to protect human health. In most countries laws require foods containing GM products to be subjected to an extensive range of analytical tests for food safety evaluation before they can be approved for sale.

In the European Union, these foods are assessed by the European Food Safety Authority. Australia and New Zealand also have a joint food authority, known as FSANZ (Food Standards Australia and New Zealand), which develops food standards and carries out assessments to ensure the safety of food. Different countries have controls in place not because safety problems have been identified, but because GM products are new and much is unknown about them. These products have only been consumed for about 10 years. The first indications from North America, where millions of people have eaten GM foods, is that they are safe. However, a variety of GM corn has been withdrawn from parts of Europe after research showed that mice fed the corn developed liver and kidney disease.

Through the Food Chain

Genetically modified foods are getting into the food chain through the food that is fed to livestock. Much of the protein found in livestock foods comes from soybeans, and much of the soybean harvest is from GM varieties. This means that animals are often given feed containing GM ingredients, and consumers are often unaware that the meat, milk, and eggs they eat have been contaminated by modified DNA. Today, some supermarkets advertise the fact that the milk they sell comes from animals fed an organic diet. However, milk and other products like this tend to be more expensive.

"It is appalling that Australian consumers are eating products which have been banned in other countries because of health concerns."

Greenpeace campaigner Louise Sales talking about FSANZ approving a corn variety that had been banned in Austria because of health concerns

"I believe quite strongly that although many consumers oppose GM crops, to improve the productivity of crops and the animals they feed, GM holds the most promise. I do believe that we need to work together as a society to help this happen."

Barry O'Neil, president of the World Organization for Animal Health

Animal or Vegetable?

Tomatoes on sale in supermarkets may contain a fish gene. Does this worry you? Some people are concerned that genes are being taken from animals and inserted into plants. For example, scientists are also working on a project to insert a fish gene into a potato to make the potato frost-resistant. Some argue that it is wrong to insert animal genes into a vegetable and that the presence of the animal gene changes the food so that it can no longer be classed as a vegetable. Others argue that the DNA of most organisms is similar and that the few differences made are unimportant. In fact, the majority of DNA is common to all organisms and only a tiny percentage is different—and this is what creates the world's different species.

The arrival of the first foods containing GM ingredients in Europe caused numerous demonstrations. Protestors asked supermarket shoppers to sign a petition against the sale of GM foods.

Food Tests

In GM food tests, a new GM food or ingredient is compared with an existing non-GM version of the food. The tests compare the composition, nutritional properties, **allergen** content, and amount of the food that is consumed, as well as the type of processing that the food might undergo. If the GM food or ingredient is considered to be substantially equivalent to an existing food or ingredient, it can be treated in the same manner with respect to safety and nutrition. In other words, it can be approved for use. If any differences are identified, the GM food has to be subjected to extensive animal feeding and toxicological (poison) tests before approval can be given.

However, the definition of substantial equivalence varies from country to country. In the United States and Canada, the presence of new DNA and/or protein does not stop a GM food from being considered substantially equivalent to a conventional food. However, a slightly different definition is used in Europe, where only highly processed foods derived from GM crops, such as refined oil, white sugar, and starch, are considered substantially equivalent to their conventional counterparts. This is because there is no DNA or protein left after these foods are processed. During processing, the plants are treated in such a way so as to separate the cellular parts of the plant from the oil, sugar, or starch. All other ingredients derived from GM crops, such as flour and protein extracts, require a full safety evaluation because they may contain new DNA and/or protein, in either intact or broken-down form. Lecithin from GM soybeans, while considered substantially equivalent to conventional lecithin in North America, is not considered to be so in Europe.

Testing New Proteins in Food

When genes from an unrelated species are inserted into a food crop, there is a risk that the proteins produced by the new gene will be toxic or cause an allergic reaction in people who eat the food. The new proteins would not normally be found in the food—for example, the protein produced by the Bt gene (see page 48) is found in bacteria, but not in crops.

Scientists carry out a series of laboratory tests in which they feed mice with a high dose of the protein to check that it is not toxic. The new protein is analyzed for the presence of any of the 500 combinations of amino acids in proteins that are known to trigger an allergic reaction. If they are discovered, the new food crop is abandoned. Finally, the new protein has to be easily digested by the body. Often, allergens are difficult to digest and they remain in the gut for longer periods of time and cause a reaction. Scientists test the proteins in a laboratory for their digestibility.

There are concerns that the new protein could react with the plant's own proteins and alter the plant itself. For example, a GM tomato with a new gene produces a protein that makes the tomato taste far sweeter. This new protein could change the nutritional composition of the food, so the new food is analyzed at the molecular level to make sure there are no harmful changes.

No amount of testing can ensure that GM foods are completely safe. However, the traditional selective breeding of new crops is also risky. Plant breeders take two plants and cross them, combining genes in a completely random manner. This can go wrong, too. During the 1970s researchers crossed two varieties of potato to produce a potato with greater insect resistance. Unfortunately the new potato had a gene that produced a large amount of a toxic protein that made people ill.

A researcher at Cornell University is examining genetically modified rice plants.

Labeling

In the United States, GM foods are not treated any differently than natural foods. Therefore, there is no requirement for food manufacturers to label foods as containing GM ingredients. In contrast, GM foods are highly regulated in the European Union. Legal regulations ensure that foods there are specifically labeled when detectable levels of DNA and/or protein derived from genetic modification are present. Food producers and supermarkets have to label foods that have been produced using genetic modified corn or soybeans. A similar legal requirement exists in Australia.

FOCUS Testing the DNA

Until the early 1990s there were no reliable analytical methods that enabled scientists to determine whether a food or food ingredient had been genetically modified. Now there is a test based on the polymerase chain reaction, or PCR. This test takes tiny quantities of DNA and replicates (copies) the DNA billions of times to produce enough DNA for analysis. This technique is also used in forensic science when pathologists take tiny samples of DNA from crime scenes. Many laboratories are already using this method to detect foods that contain GM ingredients or components.

In the European Union, foods containing GM ingredients must be clearly labeled as such. This bottle of soy sauce contains GM soya beans (soybeans).

There are problems with labeling, however. There is no single test that can be used to detect all types of GM material. Also, there is no international agreement relating to the labeling of GM foods. Even the countries that require labeling do not have the same rules. For example, they vary on the amount of GM protein or DNA that can be present in a food before it has to be labeled as containing a GM ingredient. Nor is there any agreement about how GM foods should be analyzed.

Furthermore, GM and non-GM crops can become mixed together during harvest, transportation, processing, and storage. It is relatively easy for a non-GM product to be contaminated with small amounts of a GM product without anyone being aware of the fact. To stop contanimation, a system to separate GM and non-GM products at various stages of processing would need to be set up and maintained.

DISCUSS   Should GM Foods Be Labeled?

There has been considerable debate over the issue of labeling. Food manufacturers claim that GM ingredients are no different from natural ones. For example, pure starch from GM corn is identical to starch from non-GM corn. When some foods are processed, the DNA is broken down or removed, so it is impossible to test whether that food ingredient came from a GM source. Opposing this view are the consumers who want to know the origin of all ingredients. Many consumers are not concerned when GM ingredients are used in foods, but they would like clear, unambiguous labeling to help them make informed choices. They may decide that any potential risk is small and buy the food, or decide to avoid it. Either way, consumers want information in order to make an informed decision.

In Germany there are plans to launch a "GM-free" label to help consumers identify foods that do not contain any GM products and products from animals that have eaten a GM-free diet. Producers who want to label their foods as being GM-free would have to be able to support their claim with analytical laboratory results. If you had an allergy to nuts, would you want to know if a food contained a gene from a nut? Do you think you have a right to know exactly what is in your food? Do you read food labels carefully?

"The new labeling will give consumers the choice to buy dairy products from animals that have not been fed with genetically modified plants.'"

Gerd Billen, Federation of German Consumer Organizations, 2008

GM AND THE ENVIRONMENT

GM crops are developed under carefully controlled laboratory and greenhouse conditions. However, once a new or modified plant has been produced, it is likely to be grown outside. Scientists have to determine the risk to the environment and native species before GM crops can be planted commercially.

Genetic Pollution

Once GM crops are planted outside, there is little to stop these plants from crossing with wild plants growing locally. This is referred to as genetic pollution. Some scientists predict that, within just one year, a significant number of weeds growing close to a GM crop with herbicide resistance could have also acquired this gene. This could result in the formation of "superweeds" that would be more difficult to kill using traditional herbicides. Some plants can cross with other plants more easily than others. For example, rapeseed is a crop that was produced by crossing two species of cabbage. It is the most likely of all GM crops to cross with non-GM plants.

This crop of non-GM rapeseed has been planted close to another field of the same crop. If this was a GM rapeseed crop, it is likely that it would cross with some of the non-GM plants.

Flowers need to be pollinated before they can seed. Some plants are self-pollinating, that is, their own pollen pollinates and fertilizes their own eggs. Other plants require cross-pollination. The pollen is carried by wind, water, or an animal from a flower on one plant to a flower on another plant. Rapeseed produces large quantities of pollen and attracts many pollinating insects. Crop tests in the United Kingdom found that pollen from GM rapeseed pollinated non-GM rapeseed growing more than 400 meters (1,312 feet) away, and seven percent of the resulting seed was herbicide-resistant.

Avoiding Genetic Pollution

It is impossible to stop pollen from being carried away from GM crops. However, there are ways of minimizing the spread. One is the presence of a buffer zone between GM plants and non-GM plants. The buffer zone is used to grow non-GM plants of the same type, which are harvested and then destroyed at the end of the growing season. In the United Kingdom, it is recommended that GM rapeseed is planted not less than 400 meters (1,312 ft.) from the nearest non-GM rapeseed, and that the GM plants are surrounded by a 6-meter (19.6-ft.) crop of non-GM rapeseed, to trap some of the pollen.

The pollen problem can be avoided in some GM crops, such as sugar beets, by harvesting before flowers are produced. There are trees that have been genetically modified so that they are more easily pulped and made into paper. These trees take some years to mature and will be harvested before they start to produce flowers. However, this is not possible with cereals, soybeans, and rapeseed because it is the seeds or fruits that are harvested from these plants.

RISK ASSESSMENT

Before a GM crop is planted, it is important that a risk assessment is carried out. The risks may vary from country to country. For example, in the future the tropical crop cassava may be genetically modified. The risks of genetic pollution in South America, where there are wild varieties of cassava, are much greater than if the crop was planted in Africa, where there is no wild species and therefore no risk of cross-pollination.

"Our concerns with GM trees are even more serious than crops because trees are very long lived. They are inherently geared up for spreading seeds and pollen because of the way they reproduce. There's a huge potential for cross pollination ... and widespread ecological damage."

Clare Oxborrow, Friends of the Earth campaigner talking in 2008 about plans to plant GM trees

GENE PROTECTION

The spread of genes into wild species can be prevented by making sure that any seed produced by GM crops cannot **germinate**. This could be achieved using technology called gene protector (GP), or genetic use restriction technology (GURT). GP prevents a seed from germinating. Should there be successful cross-pollination between a GM plant with gene protection and a non-GM plant, any resulting seeds would be unable to germinate. However, there is a problem. Worldwide, farmers save seeds to sow the next year. Approximately 80 percent of crops in the developing world are produced from saved seed, but the GP crop seeds would not germinate!

Many argue that seeds with GP would be no different to **hybrid** seeds currently on sale. Hybrid seeds are produced by crossing two different varieties of plant to produce a hybrid that is more vigorous or greater yielding than its parents. The farmer does not save the seed from hybrid plants. This is because the seeds produced by a hybrid plant produce plants that usually do not grow as well as their parents. Farmers who grow hybrid seeds have to buy fresh seeds each year. Just as farmers have a choice between hybrid or non-hybrid seeds, farmers would have a choice of buying GP or non-GP seeds. If they wanted to save seed, they could buy non-GP seeds.

During 1999 there was considerable outcry against this technology, especially by developing countries and development agencies, so research has been put on hold. However, this and similar techniques may offer an effective method of protecting native plants from genetic pollution.

During germination, a wheat seed coat splits, and the young root, called a radicle, emerges. If the seed had gene protection, it would be unable to germinate.

Avoiding Pesticides

Each year, farmers all over the world apply large quantities of pesticides, herbicides, and fungicides to their crops. This has adverse effects on the environment. Some pesticides kill nontarget animals and affect entire foodchains. Pesticides and herbicides can drain off fields into rivers, lakes, and streams, where they harm aquatic life. The chemicals, if not used carefully, can harm farmers. In many parts of the world, farmers do not have the right safety equipment, and their health is therefore at risk. Crops are often sprayed many times during a growing season, especially after wet weather, and the spraying is not always effective against pests such as the corn borer, which tunnels deep into corn plants.

Crops that have genetically engineered defences against pests do not have to be sprayed as much, if at all. Farmers growing GM soybeans in the United States report that they are using less pesticides. They are using one type, rather than two or three different ones, and they are not having to use the more powerful ones. Their costs have fallen, in some cases by as much as 50 percent, because they have to buy fewer pesticides. They also save on diesel fuel, which is used when spraying the pesticides.

GM crops with resistance to nematodes (tiny worm-like animals found in the soil) could significantly reduce the use of some of the most toxic and environmentally damaging pesticides. Conventional plant breeding has failed to produce effective nematode-resistant varieties, but GM varieties are being tested.

 Developing Resistance

One effect of using repeated applications of the same pesticide is the development of resistance in the pest. Some individuals in a pest population may have a gene that gives them resistance to the pesticide. This means that they are not killed by the pesticide, so they survive and breed. The gene for resistance is passed to the next generation. Their offspring survive and breed, too. The gene quickly spreads throughout the entire population.

The same thing would happen when GM crops with pest resistance are planted over a number of years. Not all the pests eating the plants will be killed by the built-in pesticide. The only way to overcome the problem is to develop new pesticides to which the pests have no resistance.

More Birds?

One of the most persuasive arguments for using GM crops with built-in resistance to insects, such as Bt-cotton, is the environmental benefits from spraying fewer pesticides. Cotton was once responsible for more than a quarter of the world's use of pesticides, and the introduction of Bt-cotton during the last decade was expected to significantly cut this use. However, two problems have emerged. The use of pesticides falls rapidly in the first few years of using the new crops, and studies have even found that more insect-eating birds populate crop fields, which leads to an increase in predatory birds, such as owls and hawks. However, in 2005 studies in China found that this reduction in pesticide use is short-lived because, although Bt-cotton is effective against the cotton bollworm, other pests are unaffected and they increased in number so that farmers had to spray just as much as with a conventional cotton crop. The other problem is that in some parts of the United States, cotton bollworm has developed resistance to the toxin produced by the Bt gene.

"What we are seeing is evolution in action. This is the first documented case of field-evolved resistance to a Bt crop."

Bruce Tabashnik, University of Arizona, who led the research into the resistance of the bollworm to the Bt toxin

Pests can reduce cotton yields considerably. To prevent this damage, farmers have to spray their crops regularly during the growing season.

Herbicide Resistance

Farmers often use herbicides that persist in the ground for several weeks to kill any weeds and stop new ones from germinating. These herbicides are designed to kill a specific group of weeds. For example, some kill weeds with broad leaves, leaving narrow-leaved cereal crops, such as wheat and corn, unharmed. Although the cereal crops tolerate the herbicide, there can be a temporary slowdown in growth. In addition, these chemicals can kill worms and other soil animals.

New GM crops with built-in resistance to herbicides may allow more effective weed control. Glyphosate-resistant crops can be safely sprayed with glyphosate herbicides. GM crops are sown straight into undisturbed soil. Farmers do not have to spray the ground before or after sowing. They can leave the weeds for a while and then spray once to kill them all. This allows insects and birds to feed on the flowers and seeds of the weeds. The dead weeds form a mulch on the ground, which helps to reduce water loss from the soil and stops more weeds from growing.

However, the use of herbicide-resistant crops has not seen the downturn in herbicide use that was predicted. In 2008 the Friends of the Earth published a report that included data from herbicide use in the United States. It showed that there had been a 15-fold increase in the use of glyphosate between 1995 and 2005. During the same time in Brazil, the use of the chemical had increased by 80 percent. There are also reports of some herbicide-resistant weeds in parts of the United States, so farmers resort to using more potent herbicides.

 FOCUS **Weeds and Birds**

Some conservation organizations are concerned that if too many weeds and pests are killed, it could result in less food for insects and birds, especially the corn bunting, partridge, and skylark. For example, most of the United Kingdom's traditional meadows have been lost, and birds and insects have become far more dependent on weeds for food. As many as 20 different kinds of weeds may grow around a field, providing food to insects and birds. Although farmers use fewer herbicides on GM crops, they can apply a single large dose for maximum weed control. Crop testing of GM sugar beets found that more insects were in the GM fields than in fields growing conventional sugar beets. The GM sugar beets only had to be sprayed with glyphosate twice, while conventional crops received up to eight sprays of a selective herbicide. The weeds in the GM field were found to attract the pests away from the GM plants, and the dead weeds provided a habitat for other insects. Overall, biodiversity was greater in the GM sugar beet fields.

Putting Useful Insects at Risk

GM crops with a Bt gene contain a toxin that kills insect larvae that eat the leaves or seeds. The larvae do not die immediately. Instead, they stop eating and die a few days later. During this time they could be eaten by other animals. There is a chance that insects that are beneficial to the crop, such as lacewings, ladybugs, and butterfly larvae, could be harmed by feeding on poisoned larvae. Research teams are looking at the potential threat to insects, both in the laboratory and in the field. Unfortunately, the results have been confusing and in some cases contradictory.

Scientists from the Swiss Federal Research Station for Agroecology and Agriculture studied lacewings that feed on the European corn borer. There is a variety of GM corn with a Bt gene that protects it against the corn borer. The researchers found that lacewings that had eaten corn borers raised on GM corn had a higher death rate than lacewings feeding on corn borers that had been raised on non-GM corn.

Scientists from the Scottish Crop Research Institute found that ladybugs fed aphids that had been eating a variety of GM potato did not live as long or produce as many eggs as ladybugs that were fed aphids from ordinary potatoes. However, another group has found that ladybugs are unaffected when they eat insects that feed on GM crops.

Aphids suck the juices from plant stems and reduce crop yields. Their natural predator is the ladybug. Both the adult and larval ladybug eat aphids. Some insecticides used to control aphids can kill the ladybugs, too.

The Monarch in Danger?

There is concern that the North American monarch butterfly could be harmed by GM corn that has the Bt gene. Monarch butterfly caterpillars feed on milkweed, a weed that is often found growing near cornfields. When the corn is in flower, large quantities of pollen cover the leaves of the milkweed, and when the caterpillars eat the leaves, they eat the pollen at the same time. Experiments have found that monarch caterpillars die within days of eating the pollen of GM corn. One of the most powerful versions of Bt corn has been withdrawn from sale. This variety, known as "event-176," produced up to 40 times more toxins than some other varieties. The other varieties appear to not harm the monarch butterfly larvae.

The colorful monarch butterfly is at the center of controversy. Some researchers believe that its caterpillars could be harmed by eating pollen from GM corn, while others claim that there is no risk at all.

"You need to compare the potential for risk to monarchs from Bt corn with the alternative, which is chemical insecticide use."

Dr. Hellmich, entomologist from the Corn Insects and Crop Genetics Research Unit, in Iowa

Back to Organic

Historically, farming was "organic." Farmers used a few natural pesticides and organic **fertilizers** in the form of compost, sewage, and manure. After World War II, the introduction of chemical fertilizers and pesticides led to more intensive agriculture—larger fields, more machinery, and higher yields.

In recent years, the effect of pesticides and fertilizers on the environment has led to a growing interest in organic farming, in which farmers use no chemicals or antibiotics. More prople are buying organic foods and many major supermarkets offer organic products. Fresh produce and milk are the most popular organic food categories in the United States.

Organic farming does not use chemicals such as herbicides and pesticides. Crop yields are lower because there are more weeds and pest damage to plants.

The planting of GM crops threatens organic farming. Current organic standards in Europe do not permit organic food to contain any GM ingredients. If GM crops are grown close to organic crops, there is a potential for cross-pollination, causing the organic crop to become **contaminated**. Scientific reports indicate that GM contamination is inevitable, so organic producers argue that they should be allowed to have a set level of contamination and still be able to qualify as organic. Foods that claim to be GM-free would need to be tested to prove that they do not contain any foreign DNA.

A Sustainable Approach

All farming has an impact on the environment. Intensive agriculture has high productivity levels, but at the expense of the environment. Organic farming has less environmental impact but, generally, lower productivity. Sustainable solutions may involve a combined GM-organic approach. A sustainable system would be one that could be carried out for many years without damaging the environment.

It could still include high productivity, a necessity given the rapidly increasing world population. For example, the area under cultivation of the tropical crop cassava has increased by 43 percent since 1970. This is an unsustainable increase because it has resulted in the loss of valuable tropical ecosystems, such as rain forest and grassland. The introduction of a GM variety of cassava with built-in pest protection could increase the yield of the harvest and reduce the need to cultivate more land.

Cassava is a staple food for 600 million people. The average yield is between 7 and 8 tons per hectare (2.5 acres), but with pest and disease control, the yield could rise to 80 tons. This could be achieved using GM varieties.

THE FUTURE OF GM FOODS

The first generation of GM crops were plants that were engineered for pest or herbicide resistance. The second generation of crops that are about to become available have been altered to supply health benefits, such as vitamin-rich rice, and wheat with more fiber to reduce the risk of colon cancer. Other crops have been modified so they produce pharmaceutical products such as vaccines and drugs. Their cultivation is called **pharming**. There are also GM crops that can grow in a wide range of habitats and be tolerant to high salt levels and drought.

Self-Fertilizing Crops

One line of research that has great promise involves giving crops such as cereals the ability to produce their own fertilizer. Nitrogen in the form of nitrate is an essential nutrient for plants. Farmers apply nitrogen fertilizers to crops to ensure that they grow well. Plants of the pea family do not require nitrogen fertilizers because they have bacteria living in their roots that take nitrogen gas from the air and convert it into a form of nitrogen that the plant can use. Scientists have located the nitrogen-fixing gene in the bacteria and are attempting to insert it into wheat plants. This process is still in the experimental stage, but if successful, it could lead to a dramatic reduction in fertilizer use, which would benefit both farmers and the environment.

Healthy Foods

A number of diseases are caused by a lack of certain minerals and vitamins in the diet. For example, anemia (lack of iron in the blood) is common in Asia, where people eat a lot of white rice that provides little iron. A new type of genetically modified rice has been produced that has three times the normal level of iron. This means that a person eating just one portion of the rice would get up to half their daily iron requirement. Every year in the developing world, millions of people suffer from blindness as a result of a Vitamin A deficiency. A new GM rice with a high level of Vitamin A could eliminate this problem.

"To dream of equal distribution of money or food resources worldwide is a nice dream but it can never be achieved... The only solution is to build in Vitamin A into their basic food and that's exactly what we are doing for 2.4 billion people and I hope that people who are so far extremely sceptical of this new technique will see that here is an example where this technique has been used for something beneficial to the consumer."

Professor Ingo Potrykus, of the Swiss Federal Institute of Technology, who has developed a GM rice with a high concentration of Vitamin A, which is currently undergoing tests

Many people in the developing world could have improved diets simply by eating GM rice with a more nutritious content.

In the future, we could be offered a whole range of GM health foods, such as tomatoes with increased vitamin content, nonallergenic peanuts, wheat with increased levels of folic acid to prevent the disorder spina bifida, and wheat with increased fiber to reduce the risk of colon cancer.

DISCUSS   Will People Accept GM Foods?

GM foods in Europe have received negative reports, and photographs of people destroying GM crop tests and demonstrating outside supermarkets have appeared in newspapers. Today, despite the fact that three GM foods are approved for sale in the European Union, there are very few GM products in European stores. This contrasts greatly with North America, where a wide range of GM foods are on sale. All the evidence indicates that these foods are safe to eat. However, recent scares related to the production of food in Europe—including **BSE** in cattle and foods **contaminated** with **dioxin**—have made Europeans wary of new foods that might put their health at risk. In addition, the environmental effects of GM foods have still to be determined, which is another issue that concerns Europeans. Europeans will need a lot of convincing before GM foods will be accepted. Meanwhile, the sales of organic foods are rising dramatically and outstripping supply.

Designer Oils

Oil crops, such as linseed and rapeseed, are important sources of vegetable oil for the food, pharmaceutical (drug), and cosmetic industries. But they could become far more important in the future when supplies of oil and gas start to run out. These oil-producing plants could be genetically modified to produce oils that are obtained from fossil fuels. The gene responsible for making a particular oil would be located in another organism, such as a bacterium or plant, removed, and inserted into the DNA of a crop plant. For example, the coriander plant produces petroselinic acid, a compound used in the oil industry. The gene could be identified, removed, and inserted into rapeseed.

Rapeseed could be modified to produce specific types of oils for use by pharmaceutical and cosmetic companies.

Biodiversity

During the last 70 years, more than three-quarters of the world's food plant varieties have vanished because farmers have concentrated on a smaller number of commercial strains. In Europe, seed producers have to pay a licence fee for every variety of seed that they sell. This has meant that they have stopped selling many of the less popular varieties for economic reasons. Once a plant variety is dropped from seed lists, it can disappear completely unless it is cultivated by conservation societies.

Agriculture is becoming increasingly dependent on a small range of crops. For example, in 1900 there were more than 30,000 different varieties of rice. Today, only a fraction of this number are still in cultivation. Many useful varieties with natural **resistance** to pests and disease have been lost.

In some countries, a single type of crop or crop variety is grown over a large area. This is called monoculture. These huge fields of a single crop are far more vulnerable to disease and pests than places where crops are more varied. It is likely that if GM crops are successful, they could be planted over vast areas. It could be dangerous to depend on a small range of crops. Climate change and the appearance of new diseases and pests could wipe out certain varieties of crop altogether.

DISCUSS   Will GM Crops Feed the World?

The United Nations estimates that over the next 30 years, the world's population will increase by 2 billion. The challenge for the next few decades is to produce enough food for all these extra people. Some people believe that this will only be possible with the use of GM crops. Other people argue that there is not a problem with lack of food, just a problem with the fair distribution of food. Growing more crops means more land and more pesticides, fertilizers, irrigation, and fuel—all of which have environmental implications. If more land is not made available, then yields must increase substantially without harming the environment. Future GM crops that can be grown in extreme conditions of heat, cold, and drought will allow less economically developed countries to improve their food security, while being less damaging to the environment and less costly to grow. Others oppose this view, stating that there is no evidence that GM crops help the environment and that in many cases their cultivation has led to increased use of chemicals. They also argue that the crops do not produce greater harvests and tie the farmer into buying expensive seed from a multinational company.

In the United Kingdom, Prince Charles is an outspoken opponent of GM technology. In 1999 he published a list of questions and answers about GM crops, which outlined how they threatened farming and the environment. In 2008 he made additional comments about GM technology, warning that the mass development of GM crops risked causing the world's worst environmental disaster and that multinational companies were conducting a huge experiment with nature that had gone seriously wrong.

What do you think? Will GM crops help the world to grow more food? Do you think GM foods are safe to eat?

CONCLUSION

It has been more than 10 years since the first GM crops were grown. There have been many changes during that time. Global warming is increasingly becoming a reality, and unusual weather patterns are causing wheat and rice harvests to fail.

People are now talking about food security. The rising price of oil, rice, and wheat has pushed up the cost of basic foods, and there have been food riots in West Africa and Indonesia and many other countries. With all the threats of food shortages, are people around the world starting to look more favorably at GM crops?

In the developing world, many farmers grow crops such as sorghum, millet, and cassava, and they cannot afford fertilizers and pesticides. They need GM varieties of their crops that will give greater yields.

Helping Subsistence Farmers

The producers of GM crops claim that their plants, due to their greater resistance to disease and pests, will lead to higher productivity. The plants also require fewer fertilizers and pesticides, so wildlife benefits. Some of the new crops being developed will be able to grow on marginal land where current varieties will not grow, such as on land damaged by saltwater after flooding. However, the first generation of GM crops are mostly aimed at developed countries, where there are economic benefits in reducing the use of fertilizers and pesticides. Commercial companies have targeted economic crops such as corn, soybeans, cotton, rubber, and papaya, for which they will see a solid financial return.

However, most of the developing world rely on staple crops such as plantain, cassava, sorghum, and millet, which are grown by subsistence farmers who cannot afford fertilizers and pesticides. These crops have been difficult to improve by conventional breeding, and they suffer from numerous diseases and pests. But they have been ignored by the commercial companies because they offer no financial return. Consequently, the productivity of these crops has increased by just three percent during the last 30 years. In contrast, wheat has increased by 130 percent. Just doubling the current yields would have a significant impact on the food supply. Biotechnology will not feed the world unless its benefits reach these farmers.

The use of GM technology in food production is still new. No one knows whether the consumption of GM foods will be harmful in the long term or whether there will be any effects on the environment or biodiversity. What is important is that the new technology is developed with care and that safety is considered at all stages. It is also important that developments in agriculture and food technology are not left solely to commercial businesses. They must be monitored by governments and international agencies, which need to evaluate the threats and benefits of GM for people in both more and less economically developed countries, and to propose guidelines for the future.

"It's good for very large agribusiness farmers, bad for everyone else, very risky for the environment, still a huge amount of unknowns."

Lord Melchett, UK Soil Association committee on releases into the environment, 2008

"GM is probably a win-win solution for consumers and farmers alike. First of all, GM is enabling farmers to grow more crops from the same amount of acreage in a world where we're struggling to feed the population. That has to be good. It's also enabling farmers to grow the crops with less use of insecticides, or fungicides or weed killers. Again, that's a green win. Together, I think it's technology for the future."

Richard Lister, a pig farmer in Yorkshire, England, 2008

TIMELINE

1859

Charles Darwin publishes *The Origin of Species,* in which he describes the process by which living organisms have changed and evolved over time by means of natural selection.

1961

Francis Crick, Sydney Brenner, and R.J. Watts-Tobin publish their theory of the genetic code.

1956–1959

Francois Jacob and Jacques Monod determine the mechanism by which genes are switched on and off.

1953

Francis Crick and James Watson publish their proposed structure of DNA.

1970

Hamilton Smith, of Johns Hopkins University in Baltimore, Maryland, isolates the first restriction enzyme using a bacterium. Restriction enzymes are the "molecular scissors" that cut DNA in specific places.

1972

Janet Mertz and Ron Davis, of Stanford University in California, produce the first recombinant DNA using restriction enzymes.

1973

Stanley Cohen and Herbert Boyer use restriction enzymes to successfully transfer genes from one species to another.

1999

Protestors destroy GM crop tests in Europe.

1997

GM food goes on sale in Europe, although it is not labeled as such.

1996

The first GM soybean and corn crops are planted in North America.

Dolly the sheep, the first clone of an adult mammalian cell, is born.

1993

GM tomatoes go on sale in the United States.

2000

The biotech company Monsanto offers the technology for GM rice enriched with vitamin for free to improve nutrition in developing countries.

2001

Researchers at the biotechnology company Syngenta publish a draft of the rice genome. The European Union votes in favor of tough rules to test and monitor the safety of GM foods and crops.

1860s

Chromosomes are seen in dividing cells, but the term "chromosome" is not used until 1888. Gregor Mendel completes his genetic experiments with pea plants and produces a set of laws of inheritance that form the basis of modern genetics.

1871

Nucleic acid is first discovered in the sperm of trout, but is not identified.

1879

Walter Fleming discovers mitosis (division of the nucleus), but he does not report his findings until 1882.

1940s

George Beadle and Edward Tatum, working with bread mold in the United States, show that one gene is responsible for one enzyme.

1880s

The American scientist August Weismann suggests that the sex cells of animals possess something that is passed from generation to generation. He theorizes that each new cell receives half the material from the parent nucleus.

1977

The first recombinant DNA containing mammalian DNA is produced.

1980

The first transgenic mouse is born. At the University of Ghent in Belgium, Professor Van Montagu demonstrates that a soil bacterium called Agrobacterium inserts its own DNA into the DNA of the plant from which it feeds, transforming the genetic structure of the plant.

1990

Professor Don Grierson, of the University of Nottingham in England, removes a gene from a tomato, reverses it, and places it back into the tomato. This change makes the tomato ripen more slowly and stay fresh for longer.

The first GMO—a modified yeast for bread-making—is used in food.

1987

The Monsanto Corporation engineers the first artificially insect-resistant crop plant.

1983

The Mexican scientist Luis Herrera-Estrella uses Agrobacterium to transfer an antibiotic resistance gene into a tobacco plant and creates the first (artificially) genetically modified plant.

Kary Mullis invents the method of polymerase chain reaction (PCR) to make copies of DNA fragments.

2006

MBASF, a German biotech firm, is given permission to carry out five years of testing on GM potatoes.

2008

The European Union discusses the relaxing of GM crop legislation to ease the global food crisis.

GLOSSARY

allergen protein that produces allergic responses, such as proteins found on grass pollen, cat fur, and certain foods

allergy extreme sensitivity to a substance, such as nuts or grass pollen, that causes the body to react when it comes into contact with it

amino acids building blocks of proteins. Proteins are made up of a chain of amino acids joined together. There are 20 naturally occurring amino acids, including eight essential amino acids that cannot be made by the adult human body and have to be obtained from the diet.

antibiotic drug that kills or inhibits the growth of harmful bacteria. As antibiotics are used more widely, bacteria are becoming resistant to these drugs.

biotechnology use of biological processes in industry and medicine, such as the use of genetically engineered bacteria to produce drugs

BSE (Bovine Spongiform Encephalopathy, also called mad cow disease) fatal disease affecting cattle that centers on the brain

chromosome one of the thread-like structures in a nucleus, made up of DNA and protein. Each chromosome carries many different genes. There are 23 pairs of chromosomes in a human cell, except in the sex cells, which have 23 chromosomes, and red blood cells, which have no chromosomes.

clone individual that is genetically identical to one or more other individuals

contamination presence of a pollutant or infection agent

cytoplasm "jellylike" contents of a cell, minus the nucleus, where proteins are made

dioxin highly toxic compound that is a by-product of some industrial processes

DNA (deoxyribonucleic acid) substance in all living things that carries the genetic code, found in the nucleus

embryo term for an egg after it has been fertilized, when it is in the early stages of development

enzyme protein produced by cells that is able to make possible or catalyze (increase the speed of) reactions within living organisms

fertilization joining together of a male and female sex cell to form a new individual

fertilizer chemicals or natural substances, such as manure, which are rich in nutrients and are added to soil to increase its fertility

gene unit of inheritance that is passed on from parent to offspring, made up of a length of DNA on a chromosome

genetic code sequence of chemical bases in DNA that code for specific amino acids

genome all the DNA sequences contained in the chromosomes of an organism

germinate when a seed starts to grow (producing a shoot and root)

growth medium solution containing nutrients on which organisms such as bacteria are grown

hybrid the offspring of two plants or animals of different varieties or species. Often hybrids are healthier and more vigorous than their parents.

malnutrition illness caused by a diet that lacks sufficient nutrients such as vitamins and minerals

molecule two or more atoms bonded together

mutant individual that has undergone genetic change that may or may not be beneficial

nucleus dense structure within a cell, surrounded by a membrane, that contains the DNA

pollinate when pollen is transferred from the anthers (male reproductive part) of one flower to the stigma (female reproductive part) of another

propagated when plants are reproduced from the parent stock, for example by taking cuttings

protein large molecule made from small units called amino acids. Proteins are important for growth and repair and have many functions in the body.

recombinant DNA DNA from different sources that has been joined together

resistance ability of an organism to tolerate something. For example, a bacterium carrying resistance to a particular antibiotic cannot be killed by that type of antibiotic.

RNA (ribonucleic acid) similar to DNA but with a single strand. It is found in the nucleus and cytoplasm, where it is involved in the synthesis of protein.

selective breeding choosing individual plants or animals with desired characteristics and interbreeding them to produce a new strain of the organism

subsistence farmer someone who farms a small plot of land that just provides his or her family with food and does not supply a surplus that can be sold

toxin (toxic) poison produced by a living organism (poisonous)

transgenic term describing an organism containing genetic material that has been artificially inserted from another species

United Nations (UN) association of the world's nations, established in 1945, with headquarters in New York. It was originally set up as a peacekeeping organization, but now there are many UN agencies involved with global issues such as food and health.

FIND OUT MORE

Further Reading

Carson, Rachel. *Silent Spring*. Boston: Houghton Mifflin, 2002.

Farndon, John. *From DNA to GM Wheat: Discovering Genetically Modified Food*. Chicago: Heinemann Library, 2006.

Fridell, Ron. *Genetic Engineering.* Minneapolis: Lerner Publications Group, 2006.

Meany, John. *What Do You Think? Is Genetic Research a Threat?* Chicago: Heinemann Library, 2009.

Parker, Steve. *Genetic Engineering.* North Mankato, Minn.: Smart Apple Media, 2002.

Solway, Andrew. *Using Genetic Technology*. Chicago: Heinemann Library, 2009.

Websites

There are many websites with information about GM foods, including those of governments, biotechnology companies and campaigning organizations. But beware—the information they hold is not always completely accurate.

www.gmo-compass.org
Website set up by the European Union with GM resources and links to stories about the use of GM foods around the world.

www.aphis.usda.gov/biotechnology
This U.S. Department of Agriculture website covers frequently asked questions, and legal and health issues.

www.monsanto.com
Monsanto is one of the leading biotechnology companies involved in the genetic modification of crops.

www.fao.org
This is the website of the Food and Agriculture Organization of the United Nations.

www.who.int/foodsafety/biotech/en/
The United Nations World Health Organization website has pages on biotechnology and GM Foods.

www.gmo-safety.eu/en/
This website provides information about the safety of gentically modified plants that have received regulatory approval. It includes a GM crop database which can be searched for type of crop plant, country, and other indentifiers.

INDEX